LEE ELLIS

Foreword by

LARRY BURKETT

CAREER PLANNING

MOODY PRESS

CHICAGO

Scripture quotations, unless noted otherwise, are taken from *The Holy Bible: New International Version*. Copyright © 1973, 1977, 1984, International Bible Society. Used by permission of Zondervan Bible Publishers.

This booklet has been adapted from *The Path-Finder*, CFC 1991.

ISBN: 0-8024-2612-3

1 3 5 7 9 10 8 6 4 2

Printed in the United States of America

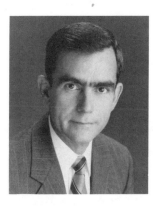

About the Author

Lee Ellis served as a career Air Force officer until his retirement in 1989. During the Vietnam war, his aircraft was shot down and he was a prisoner of war for over five years.

During Lee's military career, his assignments included duty as a pilot, flight instructor, staff officer, flying squadron commander, and supervisor in higher education. His last assignment prior to retirement was Chairman of Aerospace Studies at the University of Georgia.

In addition to earning a Bachelor of Arts degree in history from the University of Georgia and a Master of Science degree in counseling and human development from Troy State University, Lee is a graduate of the Armed Forces Staff College and the Air War College.

Career Planning

While in the Air Force, Lee became a volunteer teacher and counselor for Christian Financial Concepts. He is aware that God has a special purpose for each person. During his seventeen years of supervising, educating, and training young people, he saw how clearly God has gifted people with different talents for service in the Kingdom. Lee's gifts and experiences make him well suited for his present role as the director of Career Pathways.

Foreword

During the years I was counseling families on their finances, I frequently observed people in career fields that didn't match their talents and abilities. It concerned me that so many people were not aware of their strengths and, therefore, were not being good stewards of their talents.

I began to pray that someone would develop a program that would help people understand their vocational abilities and show them how to make the right career decisions. In 1989 I felt the Lord was leading Christian Financial Concepts to undertake this task. Lee Ellis, one of our lay counselors, was retiring from the Air Force about that time, so I challenged him to come to CFC to develop the program that is now Career Pathways.

Career Planning is a tool for individuals and families who are making career decisions. The booklet provides a wealth of information and offers many resources for making career and life decisions.

I believe *Career Planning* will be invaluable to you and your family as you seek God's plan for your lives.

In Christ,

LARRY BURKETT

Making
Career Decisions

Operating from a worldly view, rather than from biblical truth, causes the biggest problems in career decisions. In *Finding Your Mission in Life*, a best-seller on career guidance, Richard Bolles discusses the need to unlearn the errors we have learned and then learn the truths. The purpose of this section is to look at what we need to unlearn about choosing a career, then outline some steps that have proved successful.

HOW TO MAKE
BAD CAREER DECISIONS

1. Choose the first/easiest job you can get. This is the slothful way out and certainly it is not being a good steward of your talents. When you ignore your God-given talents, aren't you putting yourself in a similar situation as the servant who buried his talents (in the parable Jesus related in Matthew 25:14-30)?

Likely there will be times in all of our careers when we may take interim jobs just to put food on the table, but our goals should always be to move into areas where we are using our strongest talents in our work.

2. Choose a job based on the amount of money it pays. This error is so established in our culture, it's going to require a real measure of faith for most of us to actually choose a job on any other basis. It is the attraction of materialism and our pride that causes us to want more and more. If you haven't gone through Larry Burkett's workbook, *How to Manage Your Money,* we strongly encourage you to do so. It provides the biblical foundation to increase your faith and allow you to learn contentment at whatever economic level God calls you.

3. Choose a job because it sounds like a good title. Have you noticed how companies have changed the names of jobs to make them sound more important? One discount store calls its cashiers "terminal operators," and I'm sure you have noticed the emphasis our society places on having a good "position." Doing what you're good at and what you enjoy is usually a far better way to choose a job than just picking a title.

A friend of mine told me recently, "I am fortunate because I love my work. I have variety, I am outdoors, I get to help people, and I'm my own boss." Many people would not want his job, however, because he pumps out septic tanks. I admire this man for what he does and for the way he honors the Lord in his work. There are many people who have good sounding titles, but hate what they do and would give anything to love their work like my friend does.

4. Choose a job because your friends are working in that job or company. This is usually a trap for young people who are still very much in the socialization stage. Unfortunately, the things we had in common with our friends in school usually are not very important when it comes to getting the job done at work.

Employers are interested in your strengths, and if you are working in a job that is not using your strengths, you are not going to shine.

5. Choose a job because your parents do that job. What may have been natural for your parents may not be natural for you. In a family of several children, it is likely that one or two may have talents similar to the parents. However, differences are more often the rule. Our society offers tremendous opportunities for an individual to fully develop his or her potential.

As parents we need to find our children's talents and interests and then encourage them in that direction. *"Train up a child in the way he should go, and when he is old he will not turn from it"* (Proverbs 22:6).

6. Choose a job to fulfill your parents' unfulfilled dreams. Parents must be careful not to steer their children into something the parents would like. Career encouragement without thorough consideration of the child's God-given pattern usually causes serious stress in the child. Even though they don't always show it, young people generally want to please their parents. So if their parents are pushing them in one direction and they are naturally bent in another, the problems can be serious.

Many college students delay choosing a major and even suffer clinical depression because they are unable to resolve the conflict between their parents' desires and their natural bent. Parents need to remember they are not owners; rather, they are stewards, rearing a future adult.

7. Choose a job just because you have the minimum ability to do it. God created humans as very special and highly developed organisms, so we all have many basic abilities. There are many jobs we are capable of doing, but they are not necessarily God's plan for us. Usually His plan also involves our strongest skills, our personalities and, even more important, our motivations. He causes some areas to appeal to us more than others; these usually are related to the career field in which He would have us excel.

HOW TO MAKE
GOOD CAREER DECISIONS

1. First decide on your purpose in life. For the Christian, the fundamental question is: Do I really trust my life in God's hands? Am I willing to relinquish control to Him? Since God wants what is best for us, and He has shown us over and over that He cares, then why not let Him be in command? Why not commit to being a servant in His Kingdom for His honor and glory?

We are not capable of perfectly living up to that commitment but, praise the Lord, we don't have to. He merely asks us to commit (to make it our will) to trust and obey and then He sends the Holy Spirit to help us (see John 16:5-15).

Once you've decided on your purpose, outline some basic goals of what you stand for and what you want the end results of your work to be. You've been given talents and a life to live; this is the "so what am I going to do with it" question that will serve as your compass in life.

2. Learn about your natural bent. It includes as a minimum your abilities, interests, personality strengths, and your priorities and values. This is the primary purpose of the Career Pathways assessment—to find your pattern of God-given strengths.

3. Investigate/explore several occupations that fit your pattern. Using your pattern, you can concentrate your search on the jobs that, potentially, are a good fit. Read, interview people, and visit work sites in order to identify jobs that best match your pattern. You have nothing to lose and everything to gain through your efforts. Don't miss out on your niche because you didn't take the time to find it.

4. Seek God's confirmation. By now you should be excited about the possibilities in these occupations. Continue to pray specifically for God's direction in your search and His leading in your decision. Share your information with other Christians who know you well, and seek their counsel. Remember though, you will be the one to make the decision. Trust that God will help you make your choice. Wait until He gives you peace about your decision.

5. Choose your direction and your initial destination and develop a plan to get there. If necessary, prepare yourself through education and training to reach your goal. When you develop your talents, you are like the servants who invested their talents and doubled them during the master's absence (see Matthew 25:14-30).

6. Become a lifelong learner, always gathering new ideas about your work and its related fields. We are to study both the Bible and our vocations in order to show ourselves approved. Our society has moved through the agricultural age, the industrial age, and now is in the information age. Farmers and industrial workers are now using computers and advanced technology in order to compete. Reading, taking courses, and further training are a way of life for those who want to succeed.

7. Refine your career as you go along. After you're in a job, you'll see areas in which you can grow and develop. Prepare and move along when the doors open. Be careful not to move into an area that does not suit your strengths.

THE ROLE OF PRAYER
IN DECISION MAKING

We cannot leave the subject of decision making without a short discussion on the importance of prayer. Prayer is a powerful way that God has ordained for us to operate in the supernatural spiritual realm on this earth. When we neglect prayer, not only are we being disobedient, we are shortchanging God and ourselves of His best for us. In prayer He molds our hearts to His perfect will, and through prayer He changes the hearts of others and even the circumstances around us. We must continue to pray so that our hearts are tuned in to His message for us.

WE ALL NEED PRAYER PARTNERS

We are to pray alone but we also need to have prayer partners. We need the support of our spouses, our families, our friends, and we also need a same-sex prayer partner. There is something very special and very encouraging about a prayer partner. If you don't have one, get one, and meet at least once a week to share and pray together.

A FRAMEWORK FOR DECISION MAKING

Our Role— *Process*	God's Role— *Results*
• Commit to follow God's call	• Open doors
• Pray for His will and wisdom	• Close doors
• Seek godly counsel	• Give us peace
• Work the process	• Confirm His will
• Exercise patience	• Produce results
• Glorify God	• Glorify His name

Too often we work it backwards. We decide on the results we want and then pray that God will bless us and make them happen. Turning the results over to Him is a critical, but necessary, step if we are going to know his will.

Making Educational and Training Decisions

We live in an age of information and technology, and the amount of knowledge is expanding at an ever-increasing rate. Workers of the future will need to be highly trained and well informed. Of course, one person will not need to know everything, but each person will need to be an expert in some area and have a general idea of how to find the information he or she needs. Gaining that expertise will be very important in your ability to progress in your field of work.

Almost everyone needs some education following high school. This can come from several sources, such as on-the-job training, apprenticeships, internships, vocational or technical school, community college, or four-year college or university. This booklet provides general infor-

mation on these and lists some resources for more information on each.
Also, there are practical helps for
those considering future education.

You will find a lot of overlap in
the sections of this booklet. For instance, the information on financial
aid could apply to several educational options. We recommend you read
through every section, regardless of
which avenue of education you are
considering. In general, you'll find
that most of the concepts will apply
to your situation. You will need assistance as you plan your education.
You'll find sources listed in the following sections.

On-The-Job Training

If you decide not to pursue for-
mal education immediately after
high school, on-the-job training may
be something that interests you. This
career option does offer several advantages, including being paid while
you learn a skill. Gaining actual work
experience can be of real benefit for
you in your career as well.

**Training by an employer while
working**. There are many employers
who are willing to hire qualified, un-
trained workers for a position in

which the employee will be trained on the job. Often the jobs available are filled best by persons who have learned some of the necessary skills through high school courses, part-time work, or hobbies.

Training is expensive, so employers who invest in training employees generally screen carefully and hire with a long-term view. These employees become a valuable asset to the company.

Employers are always looking for dependable workers who really care about their work. Once you get a job, be sure you are one of the best employees in your division. For example, always be on time or even early for work. And by giving an extra effort to learn your job, you'll show that you have a commitment to the company. Your further commitment to doing high quality work will demonstrate your potential for advancement and future training.

APPRENTICESHIPS

Apprenticeship allows workers to learn both the practical and the theoretical aspects of an apprenticeship occupation by blending on-the-job training with related technical instruction. While the apprenticeship training period may range from one to six years, most trades require three to four years.

Apprentices are employed in every major industry: construction, health, manufacturing, service, and other fields.

Who is eligible: Individuals who apply for an apprenticeship must be at least 16 years of age and physically able to do the work. Some trades require an entry examination, high school diploma, or a GED certificate.

Advantages: An apprenticeship is an efficient way to learn skills because it allows earning while learning. After completing an apprenticeship, generally you are assured of a marketable skill and a good standard of living because of the demand for trained workers. Skills obtained in apprenticeship jobs often lead to important, interesting, and challenging jobs. Skilled crafts people enjoy job security, fringe benefits, and opportunities for advancement that surpass those of unskilled or semi-skilled workers.

Factors: Compare the associated job to your pattern. Does it match your strengths and interests? What are the training opportunities? What are the job opportunities? What experience may be involved?

Resources: Contact area offices of the Bureau of Apprenticeship and Training (BAT), state apprenticeship agencies, apprenticeship information centers, and local employment service offices. Check with your high school career counselor and look for outreach programs conducted by labor unions.

Check with your local schools to see if any apprenticeship preparatory courses are offered. Also, check into the possibility of credit for experience in the occupation or for trade-related skills.

(The above information was adapted from *Guide to Apprenticeship Programs*, William F. Shanahan, ARCO Publishers, 1983.)

Other resources: *What Do You Mean You Don't Want to Go to College? Turning Crisis into Opportunity for You and Your Child*, by Liliane Quon McCain and Larry Strauss: RGA Publishing Group, 1990. This book gives helpful information on how teens and parents can deal with not going to college. Other options such as work, apprenticeships, vocational school, and the like are explained.

For more information on the subject of apprenticeships, write to the following: Bureau of Apprenticeship and Training, Employment and Training Administration, U.S. Department of Labor, 601-D St NW, Rm 5000, Washington, DC 20212, or Bureau of Apprenticeship and Training, Apprenticeship Career Information, U.S. Department of Labor, 200 Constitution Ave NW, Rm N-4649, Washington, DC 20210.

INTERNSHIPS

Internships are positions that provide academic orientation and training in a work environment. Internship programs provide great opportunities for motivated individuals to gain experience and knowledge about a particular career field. They also can be a useful stepping stone into a career since many programs either hire the intern or provide important help in finding a job elsewhere.

Internships are available in many areas of study from art to zoology. The number of positions available, the length of the internship, the salary, and the benefits offered can vary considerably. One position may offer to pay a stipend (salary), include room and board, and even pay your travel expenses to and from their location. A different opportunity may only help you find a place to live.

Internship positions are open to high school graduates, college students, non-traditional students, college graduates, and graduate students.

Resources:

- Internship directories in libraries, high school counselors, college placement offices, career development centers, or bookstores.
- *The National Directory of Internships*, published by the National Society for Internships and Experimental Education, 3509 Haworth Dr, Ste 207, Raleigh, NC 27609.
- *Internships 1992*, by Katherine Jobst, published by Writers Digest, 1992.

COOPERATIVE EDUCATION

Cooperative education (Co-op) programs are structured programs that alternate terms of work with terms of instruction. They are sponsored by companies, non-profit organization, and governmental institutions, Co-op programs provide a tremendous opportunity for students to learn about the world of work, develop skills, and gain an insight into a potential career. Although these programs are most common for college level students, they also are available at technical schools.

Co-op programs are an excellent way to finance part or all of an education because the student is paid, and it is usually at a higher rate than he or she could earn elsewhere.

Co-op programs are good recruiting tools for companies. They allow the company to get a look at potential employees and even to groom them for positions in their organization. Usually there is no long-term commitment for the student or the company, but it provides both a good opportunity to check the other out. Co-op programs frequently lead to a long term-working relationship.

Considering the increasing cost of college and the increasing competition among graduates for good jobs, Co-op programs appear to have many advantages for the student. Because the student is not in school every term, graduation will be delayed one to two years, but the work experience gained seems to offset the delayed graduation.

NOTE: Most Co-op programs require completion of the freshman year and at least a 2.5 GPA (4.0 scale).

Resources: Check with the career planning and placement offices of the schools you are considering. For a brochure on Co-op programs, write to: National Commission for Cooperative Education, 360 Huntington Ave, PO Box 999, Boston, MA 02115.

MILITARY EDUCATION AND TRAINING

There was a time when virtually every young man went through some form of military training. Although there were some disadvantages to the draft, military training did provide many young people with an opportunity to get out on their own and develop maturity before making career decisions. Furthermore, the GI bill provided college and technical education for millions of Americans.

The military now operates as an all voluntary force and, as such, pays quite well, and it has excellent educational benefits. Current policy is to pay 75 percent of college tuition for active duty service members. Also, some of the services offer college funds as an enticement to enlist in needed job specialties.

Obviously, the military is not for everyone, but for many it is truly a great place to start. It does offer an equal opportunity to women and minorities that is unmatched in our society. Most important, it offers excellent training and a high level of responsibility at a young age. During Operation Desert Storm our servicemen and women demonstrated the high morale and exceptional leadership ability that young people develop in the military services. These skills help them succeed in the civilian work force.

Resources:

- Local recruiters.
- ROTC recruiters at many colleges and universities.
- Military academy liaisons.

VOCATIONAL AND TECHNICAL SCHOOLS

These schools offer an excellent way to acquire the education and skills needed to get a job in many fields of work. They generally have a good working relationship with business and industry in the local community and, therefore, provide training that is designed to prepare graduates for a specific job.

Vocational and technical (Vo-Tech) schools offer a wide variety of degrees; however, one school may not offer every possible course that is available in the school system. Vo-Tech schools are typically located within driving distance of any place in the state. Some schools have dormitories and resident programs.

Since graduates of Vo-Tech schools generally earn higher wages than someone with only a high school diploma, learning a skill at Vo-Tech should be considered a good way to prepare for working one's way through college.

Public Vocational/Technical Schools

Most every state will have a good network of technical schools. The advantage of these public schools is that generally they are much cheaper, and they are likely to be more regulated than private career schools.

Some courses of study and degrees offered at a typical technical school are shown below. Keep in mind that all schools do not offer all areas of study.

Career Planning

ASSOCIATE DEGREE

Accounting

Computer
 Programming

Electromechanical
 Engineering
 Technology

Electronic
 Engineering
 Technology

Legal
 Secretarial

Marketing
 Management

Nursing

Paralegal
 Studies

Radio-
 logical
 Technology

Research
 Lab
 Technology

Respiratory
 Therapy

Secretarial
 Science

DIPLOMA PROGRAMS

Accounting

Air
 Conditioning
 Technology

Automotive
 Collision
 Repair

Automotive
 Technology

Business
 Equipment
 Technology

Child Development
 & Related Care

Electronics
 Technology

Industrial
 Electronics
 Technology

Industrial
 Maintenance
 Technology

Legal
 Secretarial

Machine
 Tool
 Technology

Communications
 Electronics
 Technology

Computer
 Programming

Cosmetology

Drafting/Advanced
 Drafting

Medical
 Assisting

Practical
 Nursing

Research Lab
 Technology

Marketing Ad-
 ministration

Secretarial

Surgical
 Technology

Resources: For more information on public technical schools, contact the following agencies in your state.

- Nearest vocational/technical school
- State Department of Technical and Adult Education
- State Superintendent of Schools
- State Student Finance Commission (Some states have a free catalog that lists every post-secondary school, degrees taught, costs, and student population. Check your state.)

PRIVATE CAREER SCHOOLS

These privately operated schools offer training in more than 120 careers; however, individual schools tend to focus on one or two career fields, such as medical technology, cosmetology, or mechanics.

Advantages of private career schools include very specialized training and assistance in getting employment. They tend to be more expensive than the public schools, but they do fill a need for certain types of training.

Resources: The National Association of Trade and Technical Schools (NATTS) provides oversight and accreditation to these private career schools. You should carefully investigate any private school since not all are accredited. For assistance in locating and evaluating a private career school, you may want to get the following publications.

- *Technical Education That Works for America*, NATTS, 2251 Wisconsin Ave NW, Washington, DC 20007, (202) 333-1021.
- *Handbook of Private Accredited Trade and Technical Schools*, PO Box 2006, Annapolis Junction, MD 20701-2006.
- *Getting Skilled, Getting Ahead: Your Guide for Choosing a Career and a Private Career School*, by Myers, James R., Ph.D. and Elizabeth Werner Scott, M.A., Peterson's Guides, Princeton, NJ, 1989.

COMMUNITY COLLEGES

Our country offers a tremendous opportunity for higher education through the numerous colleges that are sponsored and operated by the state and local governments. These schools offer the advantage of being relatively inexpensive and within driving distance of most people.

Community colleges will likely gain an increasingly popular role in the nineties because they offer a tremendous bargain in education at a time when college costs are soaring at a rate of 8 to 12 percent annually.

Many who plan a four-year education would do well to begin their schooling at their local community college. Classes are generally flexible, allowing time for work. At the same time, their curricula is usually quite adequate for the students to acquire the core courses required by state universities.

Community colleges also offer complete courses to prepare students to enter the work force. As shown on the list below, their curricula is very broad. Some courses lead to the associate degree and others to a technical/trade diploma.

PROGRAMS AND DEGREES

Accounting

Agriculture

Anthropology

Art

Auto Body Repair

Auto Mechanics

Biological Sciences

Building Trades

Business Administration

Carpentry-Cabinet Making

Chemical-Biological Lab Technology

Chemistry

Child Care & Development

Clerical Procedures

Commercial Photography

Communications Technology

Computer Science

Construction Electrician

Cosmetology

Criminal Justice

Dental Assistant

Dental Hygiene

Dental Lab Technology

Drafting

Early Childhood Education

Electrical Appliance Technology

Electromechanical Technology

Electronics-Basic

Electronic Technology

Emergency Medical Technology

Engineering Technology

English

Fashion Merchandising

Forestry

Geology

Heating & Air Conditioning

History

Horticulture

Hospitality & Travel Marketing

Industrial Electricity

Journalism

Liberal Studies

Machine & Tool Design

Machine Shop

Machine Tool Technology

Management

Marketing/ Retail Marketing

Masonry Trades

Mathematics

Mechanical Technology

Medical Assisting

Medical Lab Technology

Music

Office Equipment Technology

Photography

Physical Therapy Assisting

Plant Maintenance

Plumbing

Political Science

Psychology

Respiratory Therapy

Science

Secretarial Occupations

Secretarial Science

Small Engine Mechanics

Social Work

Sociology

Speech and Drama

Surgical Technology

Tailoring and Fashion

Teacher Education
  Early Childhood
  Middle School
  Secondary

Warehouse Management

Welding

Word Processing

Resources:

- School career counselor
- Local community college
- State directory of post-secondary schools

FOUR-YEAR COLLEGES

Even though college costs are increasing rapidly, America offers some great values in higher education. A four-year college degree offers many advantages but is not for everyone. Four-year colleges are covered in detail later in this booklet. Evaluate all the factors before making a decision regarding what level of education you should pursue.

FINANCIAL AID AND PAYING FOR YOUR EDUCATION

There are several options for financing your education. Most people will use a combination of these options during their school years. Obviously, cost will be a major criteria in selecting the school you will attend, but we encourage you to investigate all the possibilities before you decide you can't afford a school you really want to attend.

You should also keep in mind that you can get a good education at almost any school you select. Many very successful people are graduates of small, inconspicuous colleges. College is a stepping stone; it is not an end unto itself.

Work and earn as you go. The majority of college students work to pay all or a part of their college expenses. We think this is generally a good idea because people tend to value those things in which they have "sweat equity."

As mentioned earlier, acquiring a trade or skill may be a good way to pay for college. Also, cooperative education offers an excellent way to pay for college while gaining work experience.

Parents and other family. We encourage you to sit down and openly discuss with your family their ability and willingness to help you finance your education.

For young people, we encourage this conversation early in high school so both parents and children can plan accordingly. Ideally, young people should be saving from their earnings and gift income for their future. Education is an investment in a person's future and an excellent way for parents and family to pass along some of their inheritance. Grandparents and other family members are often glad to help provide financial assistance for education, especially if they see the student making some sacrifices for an education.

Grants or scholarships. These funds do not have to be paid back. Government grants include the following.

- The Pell Grant: a direct federal grant made available to the neediest students.
- The Supplemental Educational Opportunity (SEOG): federal money sent to colleges and then distributed to needy students, based on a government formula.
- The College Work-Study Program (CWSP): a federally sponsored program that funds jobs for college students. In many cases, work-study students are employed by the colleges they attend.

Scholarships usually are based on need and/or academic achievement. However, there are scholarships available, based on many criteria. For instance, scholarships based on leadership are offered by civic organizations and businesses. Of course, there are scholarships for various extra-curricular activities.

There are scholarships for specific groups of people, including minorities. A good scholarship search will help you identify those available to you. Contact your financial aid office and your academic department advisor for their help.

Loans. In most situations, you can find a way to finance your education without taking out a loan. Unfortunately, the majority of college graduates begin their careers saddled with the responsibility of repaying student loans. As is the case in other financial areas, it's easy to get into debt, but it's no fun digging out. Many of the young couples counseled by Christian Financial Concepts are saddled with student loans and, therefore, have limited options. For instance, a student loan may require two incomes, thus precluding missionary work or the wife being able to stay at home with the children.

A good way to avoid paying student loans is just not to borrow. Seek every other possibility and allow God to provide as He sees fit. He will guide you safely through the mine field of financial aid if you will wait on Him.

Finally, if you do decide to borrow, remember the rules. Borrow only what you absolutely need; borrow for a short period of time; then pay it back as quickly as possible. Sacrifice as needed to get out of debt.

Resources:

- Financial aid from the U.S. Department of Education, "The Student Guide" outlines federally funded programs, meeting college costs, and college scholarship services.
- *How to Get into the College of Your Choice . . . and How to Finance It*, by Jayne Stewart, William Morrow and Company, Inc., 1991. This book gives tips on how to narrow the field from 3,000 colleges, stress talents over SAT scores, get recommendations from teachers and coaches, and conduct yourself in an interview.
- *Need a Lift?* A guide to education and employment opportunities with information on the financial aid process, scholarships, loans, and career information resources with addresses—a good buy at $2. American Legion Education Program, PO Box 1050, Indianapolis, IN 46206.
- *The Scholarship Book* (the complete guide to private-sector scholarships, grants, and loans for undergraduates, by Cassidy, Daniel J. and Mi-

chael J. Alves: Prentice Hall Publisher. A comprehensive directory that lists 50,000 private-sector scholarships, grants, loans, internships, and contest prizes—covering every major field from aeronautics to zoology.

Other sources of college aid information: High school guidance counselors; the financial aid officer at the college you wish to attend; libraries (ask at the reference desk for publications on financial aid); your pastor (many denominations have grants and/or low-interest loan programs for college students); your employer or parent's employer (some businesses offer scholarships for employees and/or families of employees); service clubs (Rotary, Kiwanis, or Lions); and United States Armed Forces—Army, Navy, Air Force, Marines, Coast Guard (contact your local recruiting office, ROTC department at a college, or local service academy liaison officer).

For information on work-study programs, contact the National Society for Internships and Experiential Education, Ste 207, 3509 Haworth Dr, Raleigh, NC 27609, (919) 787-3263.

Students who have been home-schooled should contact the Christian Home-Educated Scholarships Society (CHESS), Ste 576, 2008 W Lincoln Hwy, Merrillville, IN 46410.

Details on federal programs are available from the Federal Student Aid Information Center, (800) 333-4636.

ALTERNATIVES IN DECISION MAKING

There are a number of factors you may want to consider when choosing a college; some are listed below. The list is certainly not exhaustive; other factors may come into play and all of the factors may not apply to you. The important thing is that you get good information, seek wise counsel, and then work and pray through the issues involved. In doing so you are in a position to make the best possible decision.

FOUR-YEAR COLLEGES VERSUS UNIVERSITIES

Both offer advantages and disadvantages and either might serve you well.

Four-year colleges:

- have smaller classes and lower student/faculty ratio;

- have fewer classes taught by graduate students;
- are usually smaller and more personal, making it easier for many students to adjust to college; and
- can be limited in courses offered and technical support.

Universities:

- are composed of several colleges and/or schools;
- have a larger percentage of faculty-members at doctoral level;
- have lower level courses with 200 to 300 students per class;
- have more laboratories and technical equipment;
- have larger libraries;
- have numerous ongoing research programs; and
- usually have more recreational and extracurricular opportunities (but also a greater population using them).

When evaluating a school, consider your personality and habits. Studies show that students who are very organized, are good note-takers and have a lot of self-discipline tend to do well in the large classes (200 to 300) found in many core courses at a university. Students who need a lot of encouragement and personal interaction with the teacher will tend to fare better at a smaller school with smaller classes.

The bottom line is to know what conditions are like at a school. Conduct your research in the reference books and through advisors, and be sure you check with several students to find out what classes and instructions are like.

The following are other considerations:

Academic competitiveness. How well do you compare to the average student? Check your SAT/ACT score against the average for last years freshman class. Look at the percentage of students who come from the top 10, 25, and 50 percent of their high school classes. Check to see what percentage of applicants are accepted each year to the schools you are considering. This will tell you something about the academic competitiveness of the school. You might want to consider three levels of schools: long-shot schools where you barely meet the minimums; probable schools where you would be equal to a typical student; and schools which are less competitive where you feel you are sure to be accepted.

Academic major offerings. Investigate the strength of the department in which you would be doing your major course work. Does it have a good reputation? What is its relevance to the real world? Does it have good working relationships with its related professional field? What about a backup major? If you decided after your freshman year to switch majors, would you be able to get into a good program for your new major?

Coed versus single sex. Both have advantages and disadvantages. The most obvious difference will be in social life. You could consider having the opposite sex present at school as part of your social development, or it could present a social distraction from your studies. Again, it depends on the individual.

Urban versus rural. Both offer advantages and disadvantages. Your background and preferences will determine which will suit you.

Student population. Generally we are most comfortable when we are around people whose values are similar to ours. You should evaluate this area based on your own personality and maturity.

Christian versus secular. This really depends on the individual. But, keep in mind that at secular schools Christian values will not be taught. Everything should be examined in light of biblical truth. Don't give up your Christian principles just to go along with the crowd.

Conclusion. We have just touched on a few of the considerations of choosing a school. Every situation is different. These are some of the factors that may affect your decision; or, maybe none of them will affect you. You may just choose to go to the nearest school or to the only one you can afford; and that will probably work out fine.

What school you graduate from may not matter. What does matter is that you study something you enjoy and that you complete your degree. Completing what you start says a lot about your maturity and character. Having a degree not only indicates that you know something about a subject, but it also signifies you are able to set a goal and accomplish it successfully. That statement alone is usually what opens the door for your career opportunity.

Finally, remember that for most students, college is their first experience out from under the protective wing of their parents. During this time you will learn by experience; you'll make mistakes; and you'll misjudge people. You'll make friends with some only to find out later they really don't share your values, they've let you down, lied to you— even stolen from you. You'll also make some true friends who will remain close friends for life.

An amazing thing will happen during your college experience: In addition to knowledge, you'll acquire a lot of wisdom; you'll have a lot more foresight; and you will have a new appreciation for words like dependability, responsibility, accountability, and honesty. After four years you'll find out that you are a lot more like your parents than you ever thought. You'll also have a new appreciation for them and the Christian values they taught you.

FACTORS CONSIDERED IN THE COLLEGE ADMISSION PROCESS

In general, admission is based on a student's predicted ability to succeed and graduate. Following that, they look at other factors depending on the nature and needs of the institution. The following is a list of factors commonly used by colleges and universities in the admissions process.

- High school GPA (this is the best predictor of academic success)
- High school class standing
- SAT/ACT scores
- Courses taken (college prep may be required)
- Academic reputation of the student's high school
- Extra-curricular activities and leadership position level
- Character
- Communication skills
- Ethnic group
- Geographical home of student

NOTE: Schools generally have a formula based on an assigned weight to some or all of the above factors. Generally, high-scoring applicants are automatically accepted while extremely low-scoring packages would be automatically rejected. To provide a thorough evaluation and better selection process, those in the average range might receive more scrutiny and personal attention.

Hints for Succeeding in College

Assuming that you have carefully analyzed your situation and determined that you should go to college, let's look at some ways to ensure success.

1. Know your talents and develop them while you are in college. For example, if you are a people person, develop your abilities in management, psychology, counseling, or similar fields. At the same time, recognize your weaknesses; if you are weak in basic areas such as reading, composition, or public speaking, develop them to at least a minimum level.

2. Remember that one of the critical factors in the work place is the ability to think logically and critically and thus be a good decision maker. Begin developing your own theories; test them and discuss them. Take some courses in the humanities to learn about the nature of man. Don't believe everything you read or hear at college. You'll be amazed how some of the academics at institutions of higher learning go off on tangents in their thinking. Also many of them are steeped in the theory but have little practical experience. As in other areas, evaluate everything you hear or read that is contrary to Bible truths.

3. Take care of your business. No one else will look after it the way you will. This is especially true when it comes to choosing courses and making sure you meet the requirements for graduation. By doing your homework–reading the catalog and student handbook–you will know exactly what is required. In fact, these documents are the university's contract with the students. You need to know what the fine print says.

4. Get motivated; get excited about your education. A small increase in your motivation will make a big difference in your grades and your overall attitude toward college. Find some reason to want to learn the material in every class.

5. Plan your freshman year carefully. Transition from high school to college can be tough and you want to have the best situation possible. Taking calculus, chemistry, biology, and Russian in the first semester would be academic suicide for most college students at a large university. Start out with some of your favorite courses to allow for an adjustment to college life.

6. Don't get behind. Don't procrastinate. Set short-term goals and

work to meet them. Classes are fun when you are prepared ahead of time.

7. Develop a regular study routine. A proven method goes like this:

- Read the material before class. Look over the chapter headings. Read the questions at the end of the chapter. This will give you an idea of where you are going and will give your brain a framework on which to attach the important information you are reading.
- Listen and take notes in class. It will already be familiar so you will retain much from listening. Also, taking notes will allow you to visualize the information. Tape record the class if it is permitted.
- Within a few hours after class, go over your notes. Reorganize them if necessary, but be sure you review them. You have now covered the material three times and used three methods: reading, hearing, and visualizing. Later on you can review this information in a matter of minutes.
- If you miss one day of your routine, make an effort to catch up immediately. Being behind is very discouraging and causes many college

students to give up and accept terrible grades. Staying even or ahead gives you confidence and a good feeling about yourself.

8. Take care of your health. College students frequently miss class and get behind because they are sick. Poor sleeping habits and poor diet lower body resistance and invite colds, flu, mononucleosis, and other "bugs" that spread rapidly on campuses. You'll find that at least one of your friends will be up at any hour of the night, and there will always be someone wanting to do something that sounds tempting. Of course, some of those won't be around more than a semester or two, so don't let them set your agenda. Without proper rest, you'll suffer the consequences.

9. Avoid cheating—both actively and passively. Most college students cheat. You should know by now that you never get something for nothing. At best, you cheat yourself; at worst, you can be caught and severely punished. If you allow someone else to copy your work, you are still compromising the system and yourself. Remember, God searches "to and fro" for the upright who can be a witness for Him.

10. Live within your means. A few college students have virtually unlimited funds and can buy cars, clothes, pay for parties, beach trips, or whatever strikes their fancy. Unfortunately, they become the standard setters and most everyone tries to keep up with them. As in any other phase of your life, there will be more enjoyable things to do than you can afford. Develop a budget and live on it. Most college students pay big fees for bounced checks because they don't keep records, or they intentionally write checks with insufficient funds. Don't do it. It's a costly and terrible financial habit. Also, be sure you use credit cards only for things in your budget. If you can't pay your bill at the end of the month, destroy your card.

11. Actively seek a social group that agrees with your values. Your social life will be an important part of your education. Be sure the groups you associate with build you up rather than drag you down.

12. To enrich your life and help you grow spiritually, find a good church and college-age Bible study class right away.

HINTS FOR TAKING
STANDARDIZED TESTS

As part of your entrance requirements for college, you will probably
have to take some form of standardized test. Most schools require either
the SAT or the ACT exam. Furthermore, once you are in school you will
have to take many similar objective
type test. The following are some
hints for succeeding on such tests.

1. Increase your reading speed
and vocabulary. Read! Read! Read!
These tests are timed and not only
are the questions written, so are the
instructions. The tests will have many
different sections so the faster you can
comprehend what is required in each
section, the more time you'll have to
answer the questions. Many of the
math problems will be word problems
so your reading speed will signifi-
cantly affect your math score. Consider taking a speed reading course.
For most students just turning off the
television and picking up a book
would increase both their vocabulary
and reading speed.

2. Become familiar with the
type of questions on the exam and
the format of the exam. The best way
to prepare is to purchase a book that

gives typical questions and sample tests. Also investigate computer programs for this purpose. School libraries and computer centers often have them available for student use. Computer programs are good, but they should be secondary to using the books simply because the test is on paper, not computer. By working through these you'll become familiar with what is expected. You can work through the practice tests, find your weak areas, and work the review questions in those areas. This preparation will give you confidence when you take the test.

3. Develop a schedule of preparation and follow it. Several study sessions will be much more valuable than one evening of crash study. The more times you review the material, the higher will be your retention of the processes you'll need to know. Your schedule should also include limited social activities or distractions in the last few days before the test. You want to be well rested and focused on taking the test.

4. Get plenty of rest the night before the test. This is most important. You want all that information you have stored to be able to get from

your brain storage area to your conscious mind and then to your pencil. To do that efficiently, you need to be well rested. These tests are usually several hours in length and are mentally exhausting. Also remember they are speed tests and you want to be able to think quickly and accurately even after three hours of uninterrupted work.

5. Eat a good meal before taking the test. If you run out of energy, your thinking process will slow down and get fuzzy. You need adrenaline and you need it to last for a long period of time. Ask someone to recommend foods that will stay with you; avoid those which burn off quickly, giving a midmorning slump.

6. Plan to get up early enough so you aren't rushed. You want to be fully awake and feel completely in control on test day. Feeling good about yourself will add to your confidence.

7. Have a confident attitude. Everything so far has been leading up to this, because confidence is the most important aspect of test taking. Without it the information you already know will be hard to retrieve. It will get bogged down by fear or

second-guessing yourself. You want to feel so good about this event that the information and processes seem to jump into your mind. You must believe in yourself and accept the answers that your mind provides.

8. Work quickly. Go with your first impression. Change your answer only if you know for sure it's wrong. Skip any questions that have you stumped and go on to something you are more sure about. Come back later if you have time.

9. Don't expect to know everything and don't panic when you run into things you don't know. Stay in control and believe in yourself. Your continued confidence is your best asset for making the best score possible.

10. Stay organized. Look over the layout and flow of the answer sheet and, periodically, be sure you are marking the response in the proper place.

11. Keep your focus. Don't let your mind wander from what you are doing. Distractions will cause you to have to start over in your thought process.

12. Consider your personality weaknesses and overcome them.

- Some personality profiles tend to be overconfident. These people may try to wing it rather than prepare ahead of time. In taking the test, they are likely to rush ahead, not read the instructions carefully, or make invalid assumptions about the problem at hand.

- Some personality profiles tend to be too cautious and lack confidence. If you have these tendencies, don't second-guess yourself; don't over-analyze. Be aggressive. Believe in yourself. Attack each question with complete confidence. Do your best and go on to the next question. Attitude is everything. You can do it.

13. For the best results on these type of tests, repeat testing can help. We recommend that high school students who plan to attend college take the PSAT during their freshman year, then take the SAT/ACT at least once in their sophomore and junior years and again early in fall of their senior year.

14. Anyone who is considering going to college should take a college prep curriculum in high school, which is designed to equip the student with the knowledge needed to enter and

succeed in college. This is the same information being used in the standardized achievement tests. Without this educational background it may be difficult to achieve a competitive score on the SAT/ACT.

Are You Ready to Go to School?

Should you go to college? Answering the following questions will give you an insight into your maturity and motivations for college.

1. Have you prayed for guidance in your decisions regarding future education/training and work?

2. Are you really seeking God's will in your career decisions?

3. Are you sure that your friends and/or parents are not overly influencing your education and career decisions?

4. Are you considering college primarily to get away from your parents' control?

5. Are you mature enough to stick with your education/training until completion?

6. The distractions on a college campus are infinite. Do you have the

discipline to keep your focus on your education?

7. Have you developed a budget to see how much it will cost you to live on your own at college?

8. Have you calculated the total cost of your education/training and considered the various options for paying for it?

9. Have you considered the consequences of student loans?

10. Have you considered the military as an option to allow you to get further training and maturity while earning money?

11. Are you considering college primarily to meet a husband or wife?

12. Are you really academically oriented at this time in your life, or would you be better off to work for a year or two to gain maturity and direction before spending the money for college?

13. Are your talents of such a nature that you would be better off pursuing technical training rather than college?

14. Do you have a real purpose or goal for further education at this

time or would you use college as a way to delay a career decision?

15. Would you be better off to go to a one- or two-year technical/skill course and increase your earning power so that you can pay for further education (such as college)?

OTHER EDUCATIONAL RESOURCES

The following resources are in addition to those listed in each section. Most of these resources can be found in your local library or career center.

—Publications by College Board Publications, PO Box 886, New York, NY 10101-0886:

- *The College Handbook* outlines in detail study programs, degrees, admission requirements, location facilities, expenses, financial aid, and many other facets related to colleges.
- *The College Cost Book* contains data about student expenses at more than 3,000 institutions of higher learning. Also it has detailed instructions on applying for financial aid.

- *The College Board Guide to Jobs and Career Planning* describes more than 100 careers.
- *The College Scholarship Service* is sent to each secondary school in September and is available through guidance counselors.
- *Index of Majors* lists over 500 major fields of study and the colleges that offer them.
- *The College Board Guide to Going to College While Working.*

—Publications by Chronicle Guidance Publications, Inc., 66 Aurora St, PO Box 1190, Moravia, NY 13118-1190

- *Chronicle Four-Year College Databook* has information on more than 2,000 colleges and universities.
- *Chronicle Vocational School Manual* lists about 4,200 public and private vocational schools.
- *Chronicle Student Aid Manual* provides information on hundreds of financial aid programs.
- *Consider a Christian College,* a guide to 78 liberal arts colleges and universities. Peterson's Guides, Princeton, NJ.

Excellent college guides are available at libraries and bookstores and from ARCO Publishing, Barrons Educational Series, Lovejoy's, and Petersen's Guides.

For a more detailed list, check with your career center, librarian, or the American Legion publication, "Need a Lift," PO Box 1050, Indianapolis, IN 46200.

Career
Planning Resources

In your career search you will face many decisions, and to make those decisions you'll need sources of sound information. You may need to know about school admissions requirements, courses of study, financial assistance, or something about the particular nature of a career field. Getting good information usually is not easy and requires a determined effort. Normally the biggest challenge is just finding good sources for the information you need. The following are some ideas for you to consider when looking for sources.

NOTE: Although many of these sources are listed as counselors, they are best viewed as "Information Sources." We make a distinction because we believe your counselors need godly wisdom. Use these sources for information but seek counsel from those who have a biblical view of work. Godly counsel could come from a spouse, friends, parents, teacher, or a counselor who operates from a Christian value system.

FREE COUNSELING

High School Counselors

Career guidance assistance at schools varies from virtually nothing to some very good programs. As a rule of thumb, however, you only get what you ask for. That means you have to show a strong interest in getting help. Most schools have people who are knowledgeable about the college and vocational school application process. Seek their assistance but remember to weigh any specific guidance they offer regarding your career choice against a biblical perspective on work and the use of your talents.

Vocational School Counselors

Most all vocational and technical schools have a testing and counseling department to help students choose an appropriate field of study. They should be able to help you eliminate career fields that would not suit you. Their help, along with the knowledge you already have of your pattern of talents, should give you a good start in making your career and educational decisions.

College Counselors

The assistance offered can vary widely. Academic counselors generally tell you what courses you need to take in order to qualify for a degree in a particular field. Due to the large number of students they see, their help usually is not personalized. Also they get very discouraged dealing with students who do nothing to figure out anything for themselves. By doing a little research in your college catalog, you can find out nearly everything you need to know about meeting your graduation requirements. Showing up for your appointment with a well-researched plan on paper will impress your counselor and increase the likelihood of your getting some good information.

Most colleges and universities have a Department of Counseling and Testing. In this department you usually can get some free testing similar to parts of the Career Pathways assessment. Generally you will have to go through some part of the testing on your own in order to get an appointment with a counselor. That seems fair enough, yet most students will not complete the testing or make the appointment for counseling. Students can get some good information from these departments. However, their assistance generally will not look at the two most important parts of your pattern: your personality and your values. Also, it is unlikely that they will look at work and career decisions from a biblical perspective.

Vocational Rehabilitation Counselors

For those who have documented physical and mental handicaps free assistance is available, including a thorough assessment of abilities and limitations, job training and education, and assistance in job placement. Contact your state's Department of Labor or your local Community Services Agency for more information.

Public and School Libraries

Most libraries can assist you in finding career information. This could be in the form of books on the subject of job search or how to write a résumé, as well as the books on our recommended book list. In their reference section they probably have the *Dictionary of Occupational Titles*, the *Guide for Occupational Exploration*, and the *Occupational Outlook Handbook*. These three books contain U.S. Department of Labor information on jobs and are designed to help you make career decisions.

Chamber of Commerce

In your search for information you may need to see firsthand the type of activity involved in a job; or you may need to know who the employers are in a specific field of work. Your local Chamber of Commerce will have a detailed listing of the various local employers.

FEE-BASED COUNSELORS

Career Pathways Affiliates

We are building a network of Christian counselors who are qualified to assist with career guidance. Information on affiliates is included in the assessment package if there is one in the client's locale. This work will be expanded, beginning in the fall of 1992. The CFC newsletter will announce new affiliates.

Christian Counselors

There are some good Christian counselors who may not be affiliated with Career Pathways. Occupational problems are often rooted in spiritual or relational problems, which need to be worked out with professional help. Ask around in your church community for the name of a gifted Christian counselor.

Other Human Resource Professionals and Career Counselors

There are some very good career counselors who may not advertise as being Christian but who are, in fact, believers and operate from a biblical perspective. There are also some non-Christian career consultants who could be of help. If using their services, be very discerning about their motivation and values. If they are not operating from a position based on biblical truth, you could get bad counsel.

Typical Fees To Expect

Fees vary widely depending on the local economy and culture. From our experience, hourly rates range from $40 to $90 per hour, with $65 being the average across the country. That may sound high, but the cost of overhead for a small business would be a shock to most people. Career Pathways Affiliates typically offer counseling by the hour or a package that includes the assessment plus group or individual counseling. Our affiliates strongly believe that three to five hours of counseling is the minimum needed to make a difference in someone's life. Such packages, including the testing, range from $240 to $500. Considering the cost of a semester of college, a few visits to the orthodontist, a new television, or a CD player, the cost of good counseling could be the best investment you will ever make. Executive out-placement programs run higher and are priced in the range of $700 to $1500.

Career Pathways occasionally hears from people who are considering buying a career assistance program for several thousand dollars. Generally we don't think these are a good investment of your money. Ultimately you, the individual, are going to have to "do the process" of your career investigation and job hunt. Trying to buy something so complete that you don't have to put any effort into it seems unsound to us. Furthermore, the Career Pathways assessment has been a big help to some clients who had already spent more than $2000 elsewhere on professional career consultation without any real results.

We recommend you get good references for any help you purchase. With the increasing demand for career counseling, charlatans are flocking into this field.

BOOKS AND PERIODICALS

Libraries can be an important resource during your career search. Your church library may have some of the books listed on the book list that follows. Public libraries will have an assortment of books relating to jobs, work, and career guidance. Three of your most important resources, which we have mentioned before, are the *Dictionary of Occupational Titles (DOT)*, the *Guide for Occupational Exploration*, and the *Occupational Outlook Handbook*. At some libraries they may have the *DOT* on computer.

The books we have listed for your reference fall into several categories that we have found to be helpful. Obviously you won't be able to read them all, but we strongly encourage you to read through one or two from each section.

Personality (DISC)

All the books in this section use the DISC or an equivalent format to explain personality. All are written from a Christian perspective.

- *Connections, Using Personality Types to Draw Parents & Kids Closer,* Jim Brawner with Duncan Jaenicke, Chicago, IL: Moody Press, 1991.
- *Personality Plus,* Florence Littauer, Tarrytown, NY: Fleming H. Revell Company, 1983.
- *Kids in Sports, Shaping a Child's Character from the Sidelines,* Bill Perking with Rod Cooper, Ph.D., Portland, OR: Multnomah Press, 1989.
- *The Two Sides of Love,* Gary Smalley and John Trent, Colorado Springs, CO: Focus on the Family Publishing, 1990.
- *The Winning Hand—Making the Most of Your Family's Personality Differences,* Wayne Rickerson, Colorado Springs, CO: Navpress, 1991.

- *Understanding How Others Misunderstand You*, Ken Voges and Ron Braund, Chicago, IL: Moody Press, 1991.

Personality (Myers-Briggs)

Although Career Pathways does not use the Myers-Briggs Type Indicator as a part of its assessment, we see it as a good tool which can augment and validate information from DISC surveys.

- *God's Gifted People*, Gary L. Harbaugh, Minneapolis, MN: Augsburg Publishing House, 1988.
- *Self-Esteem: Gift from God*, Ruth McRoberts Ward, Grand Rapids, MI: Baker Book House Company, 1984.

Making Career Decisions

These books are from a general perspective and relate to job search.

- *Career: Take This Job and Love It*, Peter Menconi, Richard Peace, and Lyman Coleman, Colorado Springs, CO: Navpress, 1989.
- *Discovering Your Child's Design*, Ralph Mattson and Thom Black, Elgin, IL: David C. Cook Publishing Co., 1989.

- *Finding a Job You Can Love*, Ralph Mattson and Arthur Miller, Nashville, TN: Thomas Nelson, Inc., 1982.
- *How to Succeed Where It Really Counts*, Doug Sherman and William Hendricks, Colorado Springs, CO: Navpress, 1989.
- *Keeping Your Ethical Edge Sharp*, Doug Sherman and William Hendricks, Colorado Springs, CO: Navpress, 1990.
- *Keeping Your Head Up When Your Job's Got You Down*, Doug Sherman, Brentwood, TN: Wolgemuth & Hyatt Publishers, Inc. 1991.
- *The Great Niche Hunt*, David J. Frahm with Paula Rinehart, Colorado Springs, CO: Navpress, 1991.
- *The Three Boxes of Life and How to Get Out of Them* and *What Color Is Your Parachute?*, Richard N. Bolles, Berkeley, CA : Ten Speed Press, 1981.
- *Unlocking Your Sixth Suitcase*, John Bradley and Jay Carty, Colorado Springs, CO: Navpress.
- *Released from Bondage*, Neil T. Anderson, San Bernardino, CA: Here's Life Publishers, 1991.

- *Your Work Matters to God*, Doug Sherman and William Hendricks, Colorado Springs, CO: Navpress, 1987.

Codependency and Dysfunctional Family Issues

- *Codependency—A Christian Perspective*, Pat Swingle, Dallas, TX: Word Publishers, 1991.
- *The Search for Significance*, Robert S. McGee, Houston, TX: Rapha Publishing, 1990.

Financial Management

- *Business by the Book*, Larry Burkett, Nashville, TN: Thomas Nelson Publishers, 1990.
- *Debt-Free Living*, Larry Burkett, Chicago, IL: Moody Press, 1989.
- *Financial Planning Workbook*, Larry Burkett, Chicago, IL: Moody Press, 1979, 1990.
- *Get a Grip on Your Money* and *Surviving the Money Jungle*, Larry Burkett, Colorado Springs, CO: Focus on the Family Publishing, 1990.
- *Home Business 101*, Sharon Carr, Old Tappan, NJ: Fleming H. Revell, 1989.

- *The Coming Economic Earthquake*, Larry Burkett, Chicago, IL: Moody Press, 1991.
- *The Complete Financial Guide for Single Parents*, Larry Burkett, Wheaton, IL: Victor Books, 1991.
- *The Complete Financial Guide for Young Couples*, Larry Burkett, Wheaton, IL: Victor Books, 1989.
- *Using Your Money Wisely*, Larry Burkett, Chicago, IL, Moody Press, 1985, 1986.
- *Victory over Debt*, Larry Burkett, Chicago, IL: Northfield Publishing, 1991.
- *Your Finances in Changing Times*, Larry Burkett, Chicago, IL: Moody Press, 1982.

NOTE: The books listed are good sources of information for career decision making. However, we do not necessarily endorse or agree with everything expressed in these books.

---

* These books may be ordered from Christian Financial Concepts Materials Department by calling toll-free (800) 722-1976 or through your local Christian bookstore.

Career Planning

Videos:

How to Manage Your Money
Two Masters
Your Finances in Changing Times

Other Resources:

The Financial Planning Organizer
Debt-Free Living Cassette

Christian Financial Concepts

Teaching God's Principles of Handling Money

Larry Burkett, founder and president of Christian Financial Concepts, is the best-selling author of more than a dozen books on business and personal finances. He also hosts two radio programs broadcast on hundreds of stations worldwide.

Larry holds degrees in marketing and finance, and for several years served as a manager in the space program at Cape Canaveral, Florida. He also has been vice president of an electronics manufacturing firm. Larry's education, business experience, and solid understanding of God's Word enable him to give practical, Bible-based financial counsel to families, churches, and businesses.

Founded in 1976, Christian Financial Concepts is a nonprofit, nondenominational ministry dedicated to helping God's people gain a clear understanding of how to manage their money according to scriptural principles. Although practical assistance is provided on many levels, the purpose of CFC is simply *to bring glory to God by freeing His people from financial bondage so that they may serve Him to their utmost.*

One major avenue of ministry involves the training of volunteers in budget and debt counseling and linking them with financially troubled families and individuals through a nationwide referral network. CFC also provides financial management seminars and workshops for churches and other groups.

(Formats available include audio, video, video with moderator, and live instruction.) A full line of printed and audio-visual materials related to money management is available through CFC's materials department ([800] 722-1976).

Career Pathways is the career guidance outreach of Christian Financial Concepts (CFC) of Gainesville, Georgia. Since 1976, under the leadership of Larry Burkett, CFC has focused its ministry on teaching biblical principles of handling money. Career Pathways expands CFC's emphasis on stewardship to include stewardship of other talents, i.e., our unique gifts, abilities, and personal style of work.

Based on the biblical teaching that God has a purpose for each individual, the Career Pathways program seeks to reaffirm the Christian perspective by revealing how our work is really a part of fulfilling God's purpose.

Career Pathways seeks to help individuals discover their talents and career direction by providing education, testing, and feedback. More than 6,000 people, ages 16-72, have received individualized assessments through the Career Pathways program.

For further information about the ministry of Christian Financial Concepts, write to:

Christian Financial Concepts
P.O. Box 2377
Gainesville, GA 30503-2377